THE JOY OF HOCKEY

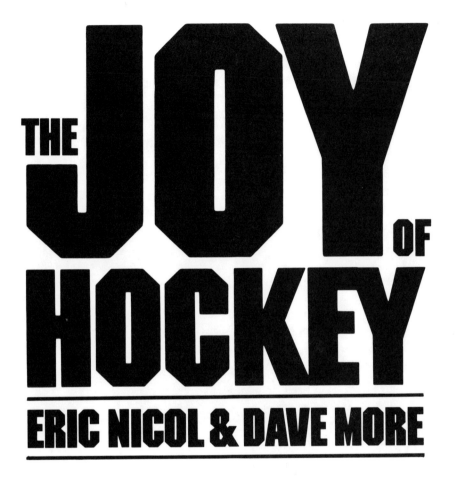

THE JOY OF HOCKEY

OF

ERIC NICOL & DAVE MORE

HURTIG PUBLISHERS/EDMONTON

Hurtig Publishers
10560 105 Street
Edmonton, Alberta

Canadian Cataloguing in Publication Data

Nicol, Eric, 1919-
    The joy of hockey

    ISBN 0-88830-156-1

    1. Hockey–Canada–Anecdotes, facetiae,
satire, etc.   2. Canadian wit and humor
(English*   I. More, Dave.   II. Title.
GV847.N53   796.9′62′0971   C78-002041-3

Printed and bound in Canada

CONTENTS

To my son, Christopher, who plays
floor hockey because his Dad told him:
"If God had intended you to buy skates
He would not have made your father
a Canadian writer."

Eric Nicol

To my friends, Rollie, Blair and
Gerald, who inadvertently posed for
most of the drawings.

Dave More

1/WHERE HOCKEY CAME FROM (ORIGINALLY)

A Knight of the Taped Lance

id Moses play hockey?"
This question is often asked by young players who are
trying to prove that hockey is a very ancient game and
therefore more important than unloading the dishwasher.
Although we have no direct evidence that Moses did play
hockey, the team he managed was on the road enough,
and engaged in sufficient violence, to represent a franchise in the National Hockey League. Thus, we may consider hockey to be blessed by God.

In more precise, anthropological terms, when David
used his slingshot to fire a small, hard, round object at

Goliath, he invented the shot from the point. He had to wait quite some time, however, before explorers discovered North America, where the ice was thick enough to support the Philistines plus three officials.

Did the North American Indians play the first games of hockey? According to their lawyers, yes. They cite the legend, which has been sustained by the Black Hawks of Chicago and other warlike tribes, that the Indian name for the game was toma-hawky. The tomahawk is defined by the dictionary as "a light axe used as a hand weapon by No. American Indians." The object of the game of toma-hawky was to remove the scalps of the opposing side without drawing a penalty. With time, the Indian braves found that by lengthening the handle of the toma-hawk they could remove scalps more quickly and also have something to lean on after their own scalps had been removed. So was born the modern game of hockey.

Attractive and plausible though this story is, it seems more likely that the sport we in North America call "hockey" is an adaptation of a sissy game called "hockey" played in remote places like New Zealand and India, on grass, with a deformed puck.

If we consult a dictionary old enough to make us sneeze when we open it, we find that hockey is defined like this: "*hockey*. (Also written hawkey, *hookey*. appar. *hook*, in ref. to the hooked or curved club) 1. A game of ball played with a club curved at one end. Also called *shinny*, *shinty*. It is played in the northern United States, commonly in winter (on ice) by a number of persons divided into two parties or sides, the object of each side being to drive the ball or block with the curved end of the club through the opposite goal or across the goal-line."

The "northern United States" referred to is Canada. We may assume, therefore, that hockey was brought over from England by former schoolboys who played "hookey" in the Old Country and were sent to Canada by their families because they could not hack it above the shins.

These immigrants were able to find plenty of clubs with curved ends in Canada, but the only grass was five feet high and full of buffalo. The hockey players experienced the same frustration as the cricketers who came from Britain because they had been told that the playing fields had an abundance of stumps. The parts of Canada that were not long grass or trees were lakes and ponds. After a few years of standing around gamelessly with their curved clubs, however, the Canadian settlers noticed a curious phenomenon. They saw that in winter they were able to walk on the water, not only because they were English, but because the water was harder than it was in summer.

The discovery might have ended there had not a Chinese workman employed by the Canadian Pacific Railway remarked to one of his English superiors, "Too bad, you cannot play glass hockey." Being bilingual, the supervisor recognized the world "glass" as the French word for "ice" (*la glace*). He at once conceived the idea of ice hockey. He organized two teams to play hockey on a frozen pond, and when it was found that the players fell down a lot without being able to get up someone devised the refinement of playing the game on skates.

The beauty of the addition of skates to hockey was that they not only made the game much faster but also

expanded breaking the shin to breaking *all* parts of the body.

Since that time, other improvements have been developed to make hockey the super-exciting game it is, or can be, provided that the players have learned how to turn corners on their skates. (Otherwise, you need a very long ice rink.)

The time clock, for instance, made an enormous difference to hockey because it enabled the referee to interrupt play by blowing his whistle and stopping the clock. Previously the players had to keep going regardless of how many of them had died from natural causes. Without the time clock, TV commercials would not be possible. Most of us have difficulty imagining what it would be like to watch hockey without the pauses required by TV commercials. They are an essential part of toilet training for Canadian children. The clock also enables a sixty-minute game to take two hours and a half.

Another development that made hockey a game rich in interruptions was the division into three periods, rather than two halves as in football, soccer, basketball, and other spectator sports. Like the three-act stage play, hockey has two intermissions during which the audience can stand up and see how many have lost the use of their limbs. In junior leagues the two intermissions also give parents the extra time they need to think about how they are going to pay the bills for the equipment their young hockey player needs in order to play the game today.

This, in fact, is the ultimate justification for

Canada's great national game: it now involves so much costly gear that it is a vital part of the nation's economy. It costs roughly as much to outfit a youngster for hockey now as it did to equip Canada's Expeditionary Force in World War I, mostly because the CEF didn't grow out of its boots every six months.

Now we shall consider some of the items needed to play modern hockey, keeping in mind that no matter how completely the player is equipped he can never replace a good, serviceable Centurion tank.

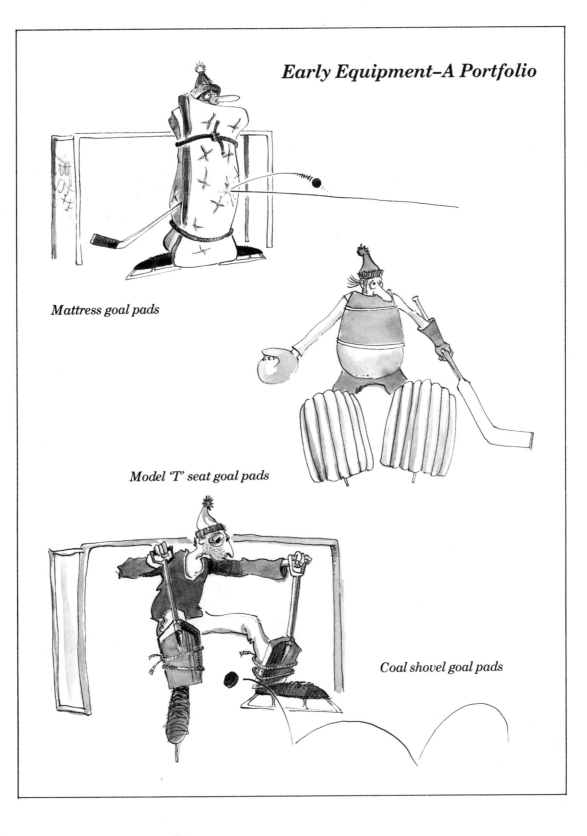

Early Equipment–A Portfolio

Mattress goal pads

Model 'T' seat goal pads

Coal shovel goal pads

Catalogue shin pads

Board shin pads

Corset shin pads

Stovepipe shin pads

2/GIRDING THE LOINS

o play modern hockey it is absolutely essential to have the proper equipment, even if you are very ugly to begin with.

The player may borrow his equipment, steal it, or, in cases of extreme affluence, buy it. But have it he must. Otherwise, he is like a bird born without feathers, attacked by the rest of the flock because he is different, with nothing in his locker except himself, hiding.

In order of importance, the items of hockey equipment are:

The Stick

It is possible to play hockey without skates, without a puck, and without a song the day would never end. But a stick is the *sine qua non* (Latin for "spear") of hockey.

Hockey sticks are usually made of laminated wood from the maple, which gives Canadian players the satisfaction of being maimed by the national symbol. Unlike the tennis racket, the wooden hockey stick has not been replaced to any extent by a metal one, possibly because wood is a warmer material with which to work over an opponent.

The hockey stick is composed of two parts: the shaft and the blade. The shaft is often blamed by coaches for their defeat ("We were shafted"). But it is the blade-end of the shaft that is used for getting rid of the puck, the butt-end being reserved for getting rid of the opponent. The butt-end is taped heavily so that the player can grasp it firmly when slashing at objects he cannot otherwise reach. The blade-end is also taped so that the player can tear off bits of tape and hand them to a linesman as tokens of his esteem, as a chance to catch his breath, or simply as something to do if the coach has told him not to pick his nose on the ice.

Hockey stick tape, which is black, should not be confused with trainer's tape, which is white and is used to hold a player together till the next of kin have been informed. A player may also be taped for presentation at a more convenient time.

In addition to being taped, the blade of the hockey stick is often curved. This enables the player to hurl the puck at the enemy like a catapult at speeds in excess of 160 kilometres an hour and helps him to remember that

Slashing

his wife takes a size B cup. Some purists believe that the curved blade complements the warped mind, and others criticize it for weakening the backhand shot. (The backhand shot is a shot that the player makes with the back of the blade, usually while pirouetting on his chin. The straight blade is preferred by older players who think of hockey as a game of skill, but young players know which side their blade is bettered on.)

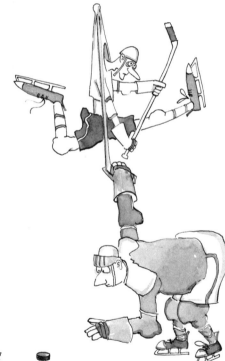

Butt-ending

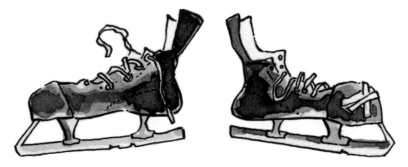

The Skates

The skates are the part of the hockey player that make him go faster than his mother had in mind.

Skates should be chosen with care, as a good-quality pair will last the young player for as long as six weeks. The reason why some parents become fascinated by the old Chinese custom of binding women's feet is that the normal development of a boy's feet stomps on his father's plan for early retirement.

Ideally, hockey skates should have blades. The blade is fastened to the bottom of the boot by rivets, making it necessary to throw away the whole skate each year. Many Canadian parents build their family planning around having three boys one year apart so that they can cut down the overhead with hand-me-down skates. Brilliant though the strategy is, the middle boy usually turns out to be a girl who needs new ballet slippers every year. Most fathers find it difficult to weld a skate blade onto a ballet slipper.

Coaches stress the importance of buying skates that fit properly. Unless the skates are snug, the player skates on his ankles, listing either to port or starboard, slowing his progress, and causing uneven wear on his tarsal joint. But if the skates are too tight, the advantage of rigid ankles is offset by the blood circulation to the feet being cut off. For this reason, parents of the young hockey player should examine his feet periodically to see if they have turned green. Green thumb indicates a talent for gardening, but green toe means gangrene. To be avoided, if possible.

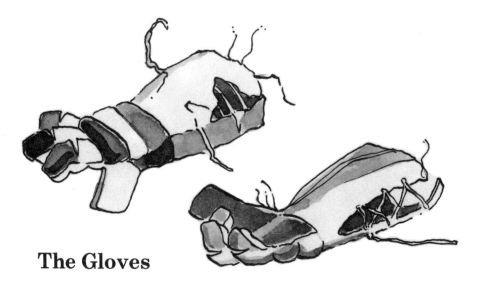

The Gloves

Hockey gloves are essential to the player because they are what he throws to the ice to show that he intends to punch out an opposing player.

The hockey glove thus has the same function as the gauntlet of the knight of medieval times, who threw his mailed mitt to the ground as a token of challenge or defiance. Slapping the face with the glove—that is, the opponent's face—to provoke a duel was a later refinement not adopted by hockey players because a good glove costs money (hitting an opponent in the face can give the glove beard burn). Expensive or not, even the most junior hockey player insists on having pro-style gloves to cast off as proof of manhood.

One of the earliest allusions to this custom is found in the *Chronicles* (1542 A.D.):

As the seconde course came into the hall Sir Richard makynge a proclamation that whosoever would saie that Kynge Richard was not lawfully kynge, he would fight with him at the utterance, and threwe downe his gauntlet; and then al the hall cried Kynge Richard.

Kynge Richard the Rocket, of Canadian hockey fame, had much the same effect on "al the hall"; nor has there been much change in the spelling ability of young hockey stars.

Hockey gloves should be a size too big, as any delay in discarding them—pulling on the fingers with the teeth, for instance—can jeopardize the future of the nose as part of the face. The strip-teaser can prolong the action of shedding her gloves almost indefinitely, confident that she will benefit from heightened anticipation, but the hockey player who delays the action will learn the exception to the saying "better late than never."

The Helmet

The helmet is a recent addition to hockey in Canada because for most players the head is the least destructible part of the body. Old-time hockey players protected their elbows with pads, since much of their life off-ice depended on bending the elbow. The head, however, they considered to be expendable. They wore their welts proudly, as the Prussian calvarymen did their duelling scars. Nor did they worry about losing an ear, knowing that whoever found one would return it (the honour system).

The helmet is, in fact, still disdained by some Canadian hockey players because the strap interferes with chewing gum. European players, who do not chew gum, nor indeed chew anything to strengthen their jaws for close combat, all wear helmets. This is a particularly strict rule for players from communist countries such as

Russia and Czechoslovakia where a skull fracture is classed as a serious injury.

Canadian junior players, however, are learning to like the helmet, having found that it provides extra impact when butting an opponent. Butting is an underrated skill of hockey. It is used most often when an opponent has pulled a player's sweater over his head so that he is in effect playing in complete darkness. For some players this is a handicap. As an aid to the handicapped, therefore, the helmet is useful in butting out of the way objects that are detrimental to good vision.

While insisting on the helmet for younger players, the Canadian Amateur Hockey Association frowns on the model topped by a spike in the style of the German army helmet of World War I. The foreseen hazard is that a player sliding out of control might impale himself on the boards and have to have his prong amputated, thereby

delaying the game. Because hockey is known as the fastest game on two feet, any refinement in the player's apparel must be such that a linesman can still pick up an object with one hand while skating at top speed and without doubling the length of his arm. This rules out not only the heavier helmet—with or without beaver—but also chain-mail pants, buckler, carapace of steel, and any other armour for which a crane must be used to hoist the player onto his skates.

The exception to this rule is the hockey helmet that includes a face mask. The face-mask helmet is worn by peewees to whom the extra weight doesn't matter because they already fall down a lot. Intended to save the face in case the player wants to use it for something other than hockey, the face mask puts the wearer at a disadvantage in that he loses some of his peripheral vision and thus becomes more vulnerable to a body check that may destroy his knees. The hockey player must therefore, make up his mind, before he starts, about which parts of his body he wants to save for his later years—a nice face and no knees, or nice knees and a lot of dinners by candlelight.

The Goalie's Gear

The goalkeeper wears a mask as a reasonable alternative to exchanging his head for a pound of ground round.

Developed beyond the merely functional, the netminder's mask of today is designed and painted to resemble closely the masks of the head-hunters of New Guinea (whose application for a franchise in the NHL has yet to be approved). The more grotesque the goalie's mask, the better his chances of warding off evil spirits (Philadelphia).

The keeper of the goal is seen as the central figure—the soul, if you like—of the hockey team, and his fetish of wearing a unique and frightening mask helps him to fulfill the role of shaman or medicine man, give or take a few bear claws. It is only a matter of time, therefore, till the New York Islanders' goalie adds a necklace of clam shells.

It was the custom of west coast North American Indian tribes for the chief to carry a "talking stick." The masked goalie also carries a talking stick, which he uses to say a good deal, especially to an opposing player who tries to park himself inside the goal crease. The goalie may also use the stick to try to stop the puck from entering the net, but more often he will use his glove, his blocker, his pads, his skates, or any portion of his torso that he does not expect to need for a couple of months.

The goalie employs his glove to catch the puck when playing at home and his blocker to deflect the puck into the crowd when he is playing in the opponent's rink. Indeed, although his shield is a bit smaller and his spear not quite so sharp, the modern, fully-equipped goalie is a match for the Zulu warrior as a fierce demon of doom.

Hence the tribal custom in which the other players of the team, before each period, skate past their goalie to touch his pads with their sticks and become imbued with his power to destroy.

The talking stick

Undies

Very little is known about what hockey players wear under their ceremonial attire. It is believed that they do wear something, but a precise inventory has never been reported. The only substructure visible to the patron is the heavy braces and padding revealed in the course of a brawl. Although Canadians seem to be aroused by this glimpse of the hockey player's foundation garments, his costume as a whole must be rated as the least erotically stimulating in all sport. Short or tight pants are worn by players of football, soccer, basketball, and tennis. Only the hockey player looks as though he has been sifted into boxer shorts tailored for King Kong and overlapped by a sweater knitted by the Madwoman of la Place de la Concorde.

It is perhaps because of the unflattering apparel worn in hockey that baseball is known as a game played by curved girls with a straight stick and hockey a game played by straight boys with a curved stick.

The Puck

Sometimes used in a hockey game, the puck is a disc of hard rubber held sacred by orthodontists.

The puck differs from other missiles used in games—i.e., the baseball, football, badminton shuttle, etc.—in that holding it is against the rules. This is what makes hockey popular with so many Canadian parents—they know that their son is chasing something he can't put his hands on. It is also reassuring to them that the boy is going to the drugstore to buy a rubber object that may be autographed by Bobby Hull.

This is all the equipment needed to play ice hockey, unless the player's number is 007.

3/THE RULES
OF HOCKEY
(IF ANY)

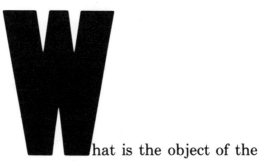

hat is the object of the game of hockey? Is it to have fun? Is it a way of keeping warm in winter without adding to the drain of fossil fuels? Is it the best means of making sure that parents of young hockey players have no money left to squander on frivolous items such as food and shelter?

No. The purpose of hockey is to *win*. Other sports afford the player an opportunity to get out in the fresh air and sunshine so that winning, while desirable, is not the essence. Hockey is played mostly indoors, in smoke-filled arenas and at a temperature whose only physical benefit is that it freezes the gums before the teeth are extracted. For this reason, the hockey team that fails to win has wasted its time. It got all dressed up for nothing.

Accordingly, the rules of hockey may be divided into (a) rules that help you win and (b) rules that do not help you win.

To understand both kinds of rules, first we must know something about the field of play, which includes the ice area and the first six rows of seats into which a player may be body-checked. The ice itself varies in length and width, the North American ice being smaller than the European so that the players will not have to skate as far in order to knock one another down.

How thick should the ice be? This question is often asked in isolated communities where the refrigeration equipment consists of getting the cold shoulder from the town council. Generally speaking, the ice for hockey should be thick enough that it will not melt down to the concrete on the spot where Bobby Clarke is explaining to the referee, in his own words, the inherited social disease responsible for the official's loss of eyesight.

At each end of the ice is a goal. This goal is not as large as a soccer goal, unless you are playing against the Montreal Canadiens, in which case your goal may expand beyond regulation size.

The hockey goal sits on two steel pins which are useful to the goalie in that the referee must stop play if the

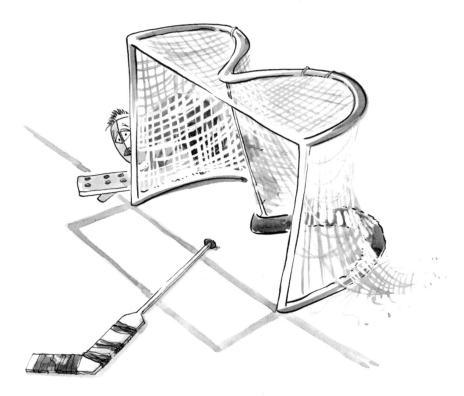

goal is knocked off its pins. At times when the goalie is
hard pressed, strange seismic forces can knock the goal off
its pins and are often the first indication that the region
has a geological fault. Some goalkeepers explain the phenomenon as a form of psycho-kinesis—the power to move
any object smaller than Kate Smith simply by thinking
about it. This power is vested in someone outside the
play, such as the trainer's grandmother. To exorcise the
demon responsible for such unaccountable acts as the

shifting of the goal off its supports requires at least two priests and an usherette.

In line with the goal posts is the goal line. This is probably the most important line in hockey outside the player's contract. Since the object of the game (winning) cannot be attained without putting the puck across your opponent's goal line more often than he puts it across yours, the goalie must guard the line with his life or, better still, the life of an opposing player.

If, while playing even sides, a player shoots the puck from his own end of the ice across the opponent's goal line but not into the goal, and an opposing player touches the puck first, the play may be whistled down for the in-

fraction called "icing the puck." Icing is frowned on because it helps to relieve the pressure on a defending team,
and it is not considered to be in the best interest of a
spectator sport such as hockey to relieve any pressure
other than that of thumbscrew or iron maiden.

The punishment for icing the puck is having to take
a face-off in your own end. What is a face-off? A face-off is
a face that by one means or another has been taken off.
The elbow is a favoured instrument for this operation. In
addition, the face-off is a way of putting the puck into
play without a formal declaration of war. The procedure
is as follows.

Two opposing players chosen for their skill in winning the face-off confront each other like fencers but with
the blades of their weapons on the ice. When the official
drops the puck between them, the players ignore it and
slash at each other vigorously, at the same time trying to
kick the puck to a teammate. Winning the face-off requires excellent co-ordination of eyes, hands, and feet,
similar to the kind developed by the Canadian farm boy
in the barn shovelling up droppings behind a very mean
mare.

The face-off may be at centre ice or in any of the circles except the circles under the coach's eyes. These
charmed circles (or fairy rings) have the purpose of keeping out players not immediately concerned with the fate
of the puck. The players lined up around the circle oc-
cupy themselves with creative jostling. This involves

using the butt-end of the hockey stick to do exploratory surgery between the short ribs.

If one of the players taking the face-off moves before the puck is dropped, he may be waved out of the circle by the official, a mortifying experience that may darken the rest of his days if he is already a little depressed.

A face-off may also be called outside the circle if the puck goes over the boards or if the referee has reason to believe that nobody knows where it is. In such an event the players line up around an *imaginary* circle. Fortunately this is the only time in playing hockey when you need to use your imagination. If this should give you a headache, or aggravate a tendency to bedwetting, you might be wise to switch to another game in which the lines are clearly visible at all times.

Two other lines in hockey—more reliable in that they are straight lines and extend the full width of the ice—are *the blue lines*. These blue lines should not be confused with the blue lines overheard by roving microphones during "Hockey Night in Canada." The latter type of blue line has only recently come to public notice since in the past the viewers of hockey games have assumed that what the good, clean Canadian lads were exclaiming was "Shucks!" or, if unduly provoked, "Oh fudge!" A European lip-reader, after watching his first game of hockey, expressed surprise that all Canadian hockey players were called Atholl. Modern sound equipment, moreover, has made evident that the Lady Byng Trophy for most sportsmanlike player was awarded because Lady Byng was deaf.

Such equipment is not needed for the non-verbal blue line, which tells the player when he is off-side. Being off-side is a situation of shame. A player may get a girl into trouble and be excused, but when he gets his whole team into trouble by putting himself off-side he commits a mortal sin.

A player is called off-side when he precedes the puck across the opponent's blue line. As this stops the play and nullifies the rush, the player must do everything possible to ensure that, regardless of where the rest of his body is in the arena, one foot remains on the line till the puck has crossed it.

The player is also off-side if a teammate passes the puck across his own blue line and the red line, but there is less guilt attached because it is not clear which player is to blame. In Japanese hockey, hara-kiri is optional after a two-line pass.

The red line is the line marked across the centre of the ice so that a player will know where the middle is, assuming, that is, that the player makes some effort to keep himself informed. The player who is unable to distinguish between the red line and the blue line, especially if he has been playing hockey long enough to be drafted into the NHL, should have his attention span checked. Generally speaking, if the player has learned to wave bye-bye, he should be able to locate the red line. If he persists in getting the lines mixed up, he should tell the coach that he is colour blind. He can then add substance to the excuse by driving his car through a few red lights. Nobody wants to look foolish.

Besides the infractions of the rules that result from ignoring the lines, a player may be charged with the more serious offence called a *penalty*. In most other games when a player is sent off the field of play, he is not allowed to return till the game is over and so he can have little effect on the outcome. In hockey, however, there are so few players to a side (six) that when one of them is banished his absence is almost immediately noticeable.

Staying onside

Therefore, a player is permitted to rejoin his teammates after serving time in the penalty box for two minutes (minor penalty), five minutes (major penalty), ten minutes (very major penalty, or misconduct), or fifteen years (assault with a deadly weapon). The lesser penalties are assessed by the referee, who wears an armband out of respect for the deceased. Any penalty over six months is given by a provincial court judge, who wears a black robe in order to impress upon the accused that braining another hockey player is almost as serious as assaulting a human being.

Hockey coaches divide penalties into two kinds: (a) "bad" penalties and (b) "good" penalties. (Note: the venialness of hockey penalties meriting only temporal punishment is a subject for abstruse philosophical debate beyond the scope of this work.)

A bad penalty is a penalty incurred by a player while his team has the puck or is considering getting it. A penalty is considered good when incurred while the other team has the puck and seems determined to do something with it. Receiving a penalty just as the opposing player is about to put the puck into the net is extremely good, indeed almost saintly.

The penalties, both good and bad, are the most extensive of any physical contest since the Inquisition. They include charging, boarding, tripping, spearing, high-sticking, elbowing, slashing, delaying the game, and a variety of other offences grouped under "interference." (If

Delaying the game

Brutus and the other conspirators who stabbed Julius Caesar at the forum had been on skates they would have been charged with interference.)

Most of these penalties are minor, costing the player two minutes in the penalty box (also known to hockey buffs as "the sin bin," "the goon gazebo," etc.). Because of the profusion of penalties that hockey offers to the player naturally endowed with violence, it is sometimes difficult for the referee to make the distinction between a minor penalty such as "roughing"—the term used to describe hitting a player in the face with the fists—and a major penalty such as "fighting"—used to describe hitting a player in the face with the fists enough times to suggest that it involved an element of ill feeling.

A similar overlap exists between "hooking"—another minor infraction—and gaffing and filleting, which for some reason are omitted from the rule book.

Equally regrettable is the penalty known as "deliberate attempt to injure." The player who is hitting another player in the face with his fists or is pulling his hair out by the roots is not considered to be deliberately attempting to injure because the work is all hand-done. If he breaks his stick over his opponent's head, however, and especially if he uses the kindling to cremate the body, the referee may at his discretion judge it to be a deliberate attempt to injure.

The referee may also escalate a minor penalty to a major penalty if the player has drawn blood. It doesn't need to be much blood. As long as the victim can show the referee some blood that is not actually in a Red Cross bottle, there is a good chance that his assailant will spend five minutes in Coventry. For this reason, a player can help his team if he bleeds easily. He need not be an actual hemophiliac—this would run up the laundry bill for towels—but a lively trickle when clipped with a high stick is one way of using his head when its other functions have failed.

The penalty for these homicidal attacks is called a "misconduct." A misconduct is the strongest penalty term in hockey. For comparison, we may think of the sacking of Troy as a misconduct. (The massacre of General Custer and his troops was not a misconduct—it was over too fast.)

In hockey a player may receive a five-minute misconduct, a ten-minute misconduct, or a game misconduct; the last of these means his banishment from the game and the payment of a fine (known to the players' association as cruel and unnatural punishment). A player may receive a game misconduct for chopping down a standing official or for making an obscene gesture at the crowd.

What is an obscene gesture? Coaches are often asked this question by young players who are afraid that one or more of their fingers has a dirty mouth. Rather than take a chance the player will tape his hands so that the fingers

Clearing the bench

have nothing to say. He should be made to understand, however, that twiddling the fingers at the nose is no longer considered to be an obscene gesture, except in remote areas that lack secondary schools. He may have to be taught the names of the fingers—Thumbkin, Pointer, Middle, Ring, and Pinkie—to facilitate his remembering which is the troublemaker. And, he can be instructed never to raise the fingers above the shoulder unless he has to go to the bathroom.

Besides having to take the penalty for an obscene gesture, a way of being sent to the showers early is to be the "third man in" during an altercation. This rule was instituted because a player sometimes rushed to the rescue of a teammate who was being pummelled unmercifully. His joining the fray led to "clearing the benches," a procedure in which all the players of both teams swarm onto the ice, grab a partner of approximately the same size, and mill around in a sort of clumsy version of The Great Waltz.

Spectacular though the scene is, hockey authorities deplore it, not only because it is difficult for two linesmen to cut in between ten or fifteen waltzing couples at the same time, but also because it complicates the phasing in of TV commercials. It is almost impossible to choreograph this number of infuriated men so that they pause in dismantling one another while the viewer watches a message for preventive maintenance. Hence the severe punishment for the player who puts the survival of a teammate ahead of the sponsor's product.

Because hockey players can receive only so many stitches in a given game, there are a few penalties which are not related to physical violence. A "bench penalty," for example, does not mean that the bench has to go to the penalty box (there is already a bench in there), but is a penalty called by the referee to blow down the coach who is standing on the bench voicing oddities about the official's sex life that are not listed in the souvenir program.

The name for this infraction is "unsportsmanlike conduct." Conduct that is considered to be unsporting covers a wide variety of gestures and utterances with which a member of a team indicates that he does not have a fatalist's attitude toward the slings and arrows of outrageous fortune. Among the ways of being unsportsmanlike are: slamming the stick against the boards, kicking shut the penalty box gate so hard that the false teeth jump out of the mouths of oldtimers in the first five rows, and—most vehement of all—spitting.

It is possible to write a whole chapter on the importance of spitting in hockey. With the possible exception of semi-professional baseball in the southern United States, no game glorifies expectoration more than our grand national sport. Its manliness, its élan, its lyricism—all are in the hockey spit.

This does not mean that a player has no future in professional hockey if for some reason he has a spitting deficiency. Sometimes a simple operation will correct a weakness of the salivary glands. If the player still spits without distinction, he can try to emulate the gentlemanly Jean Beliveau and play the game without oral ejaculation. But it will not be easy. A player who expresses his disgust by raising an eyebrow rarely wins the adulation of a crowd that has come to watch the raw, and moisturized, play of primitive emotion. His teammates may also be leery of him, as a dry mouth is associated with anxiety whereas the ample jet of juice—ideally tobacco-stained—bespeaks the cold fury of the completely self-assured psychopath.

Besides exuding this emotive quality of spitting, the hockey player with a gap between his remaining teeth can reach heights of artistry unique to the game. The curve spit, the sinker, the deflection—these and more water the laurels of the Compleat Hockey Player.

Accepting a penalty

Should the player ever accept his penalty or other abuse graciously? Answer: never. No matter how deserved the penalty, the player *must* make it plain to all present that his wrath has surmounted the obstacle of common civility. Even when he is taking a "good" penalty, the star player portrays martyrdom, taking the lumps deserved by others. Such a response is essential to show that the player has *"become involved."*

To become involved in hockey has a meaning somewhat different from that of the phrase as applied to Canada's other popular contact sport. The junior player can go home and tell his mother "Mom, tonight I got involved," and his mother will be delighted, once he has stopped hemorrhaging.

When a player becomes involved, he goes a long way toward making up for being unable to skate or shoot. But his coach will be even happier if he can become involved while scoring a goal. Despite the catechism of hockey—"To beat them on the ice, first must thou lick them in the alley"—taking penalties is not the entire game. Indeed, in order to win, the team must either score more goals than the opponent or win by default because the other team fails to show up. (The special techniques of ensuring that the other team does not show up, such as filing the steering cable of the team bus, will not be dealt with in this treatise.)

So, how is a goal scored? Usually, a goal is scored when the puck enters the net after crossing the goal line.

The best place for this to happen is at the front of the net, as the player who tries to push it through from behind will be hindered by the mesh which has been made too small for the puck to pass through without some very deft foreplay with scissors.

Occasionally, a goal is scored when the puck has not entered the net or is not scored when it has. These irregularities may be attributed to the speed with which the puck sometimes travels (two hundred kilometres an hour), the erratic flight of the rubber disc, or a momentary lapse of attention on the part of the goal judge, such as his going out for a hot dog.

When the goal judge has the impression that the puck has entered the net, he pushes a button that turns on the red light. (It is important that the goal judge, as a person sitting in a window under a red light, does not wear too much lipstick.) The activation of the red light may be questioned by players who try to improve the goal judge's vision by breaking the glass with their sticks. In such delicate situations the referee has the final decision on whether there has been a goal, a no-goal, or a case for the United Nations.

In addition to the red light, hockey has the green light operated by the timekeeper to signal the end of each period. The periods, of which there are three in regulation time, are each of twenty minutes' duration, but a period runs considerably longer than that because the clock stops when the old man dies or when the referee blows his whistle, whichever comes first. As a result, the clock is an extremely important part of hockey. Coaches and players alike stare up at it with a reverence rarely seen outside the Sistine Chapel.

Scoring on a deflection

At the risk of becoming walleyed, the hockey player keeps one eye on the clock so that he knows how much time is left in the period, how much time is left in a penalty, and how much "ice time" he is getting (as opposed to "bench time," "lunch time," and "time to go sleepy-sleeps.")

For this reason, it is desirable, though not obligatory, that the hockey player be able to tell time. In the heat of the action the coach is too pressed to be able to point out to a player—especially a player on the ice—that the hockey clock runs backwards, unlike the digital clock he got for Christmas, and he must adjust to the time warp without waiting to be launched into space.

Other incidents that may stop the clock include—

(a) knocking down the puck with a high stick

(b) knocking down a player with a high stick

(c) playing "knock, knock, who's there?"

(d) throwing onto the ice of programs, live squid, dead chickens, and similar objects not on the club roster

(e) melting of the ice (if accompanied by the appearance of a Great Lakes freighter)

(f) sudden conversion of the official timekeeper to Zen Buddhism.

In addition to these important rules, hockey has a number of picky, picky, picky rules that may be necessary but are not much fun at a party.

For instance, a player may have his stick challenged

by an opposing team for having too big a wow in the hook. The player's mind may be as warped as suits him, but if his stick is more than one kilometre out of line he is penalized for playing the wrong game (jai alai) and sent to Mexico. If on the other hand his stick, when measured by officials, is found to be deformed within the legal limit the opposing team is fined for delaying the game and making the referee put on his glasses.

The same penalty is assessed for wrongfully casting an aspersion on the width of the goalie's pads. The insinuation is that the goalie—usually a Canadian from a God-fearing family and a little house on the prairie—has donned pads wider than six feet because persons of evil intent have seduced him with the proposition that the wider the pads the less the chance that the puck will find its way into the net. Since his pads are the most sensitive part of a goalie's body, the ritual of measuring them causes strong men to avert their eyes and women to clutch their children to their breasts. Regardless of how one feels about the divinity of Christ, to doubt a goalie's pads is an act of desperation in Canada, and should be treated with the contempt it deserves.

Some Punishable Infractions

Boarding

Roughing

Hooking

Holding

Tripping

Fighting

4/SKILLS
(&OTHER GOOD
THINGS TO HAVE)

The dreaded hipcheck

n hockey the main difference between a rule and a stick is that when a player breaks a rule he cannot skate to the bench and get a new one. To break a rule accidentally is unforgivable. The state of innocence does not exist in hockey, unless the team lacks proper coaching.

In addition to this basic knowledge, the player should have certain skills. For example, he should know how to skate. Any hockey player over the age of twenty who has not learned how to skate and who has been unable to progress beyond the minor league should ask himself seriously whether he could not be more fulfilled playing some other game where ice is more occasional.

Skating, of all the skills in hockey, requires a certain *physique*, the medical term for public parts of the body as opposed to those you usually play with.

The Hockey Physique

First, the legs. Ideally, the hockey player has two legs. Cases of one-legged hockey players have been recorded, but these are the exception. The person with an artificial leg who is courageous enough to try to play hockey deserves our admiration and applause so long as he doesn't persist in turning out for our team, in which case he should be discouraged with a kick in his good shin.

Good legs are desirable in skating, as everyone knows who has watched the Ice Capades. When the skater is playing hockey, however, dimpled knees do not count for as much. In fact, many hockey players' knees are downright ugly because they have had a cartilage removed. The likelihood of this type of damage being caused by hockey makes it a definite advantage to have knees with extra cartilage so that a damaged one won't be missed.

Is it a handicap to have short legs? It is a common belief among hockey parents that the longer leg affords a longer stride when skating as well as a wider radius for tripping and kneeing. They urge their offspring to engage in leg-lengthening exercises such as sleeping suspended by the ankles from the ceiling. They may also fortify his diet with elements favoured by the ostrich—fruit, seeds, and small reptiles—in hopes that he too will be capable of ninety kilometres an hour on the flat.

The truth, however, is that many of the best hockey players have stocky legs. This feature allows the time required for messages to travel from the brain to the feet to be short enough to assure same-day delivery. Also, a mist has sometimes been known to form over the ice surface, and the tall player whose head projects above the fog may be playing at a distinct disadvantage unless he has been wired for instrument take-off and landing.

That runty pegs are no hindrance to speed on the ice is shown by the superiority of the French Canadian as skater. Most Canadiens are of compact design. Their ability to change direction instantly is, it is true, the result of

A message from the bench

years of training as pedestrians in Montreal traffic. But even if they had never had specialized instruction in sharing the sidewalk with a French cab driver, they would be remarkably agile for their height, weight, and volume. (Note: there is no clinical proof that the secret of the French-Canadian hockey player's success is that his centre of gravity is close to a decent restaurant.)

The only other physical distinction in hockey players is that defencemen are usually larger than forwards because a defenceman must use his body to stop things—players, pucks, fights, etc.—and the more body he has, the better his chance of having some of it left to take home after the game.

As the defenceman also must skate backwards a good deal it helps if his knees bend both ways. But this aptitude depends, as a rule, on how often his team plays against Philadelphia. What matters more is his bulk since this enhances the most respected skill in hockey—

Hitting

Hitting means something different in hockey than it does in baseball. In baseball a "hit" is scored when the bat connects with the ball in such a way that the batter is able to reach one or more bases before the fielding team can put him out. But the hockey player can score a hit and put his opponent out at the same time, without even touching the puck. He does this by colliding violently with the player who either has the puck or knows where it was last seen.

This hit is called a *bodycheck*. There are various ways to check a body (besides reading the tag on the toe), but the general purpose is to "take the man out." Even more than taking a woman out, taking a man out is contact sport at its best so long as fertilization does not take place.

The simplest way to body check is to squeeze the opposing attacker against the boards till his body becomes part of the grain. Not much finesse is needed for this manoeuver, based as it is on the simple physics of two objects occupying the same space at the same time without changing their molecules.

More spectacular is the dreaded *hipcheck*. This hit is executed by a player throwing his hip sideways, in a motion redolent of the hula movement representing the Hawaiian god of hospital insurance. Timed correctly, the hipcheck causes the onrushing opponent to cartwheel to a halt and perhaps give serious consideration to a career in basket weaving. Some players take offence at being hipchecked, despite its being legal, and they seek revenge by breaking their sticks over the hipchecker's head. This does not affect the end of the spine that has the talent, however, and hipcheckers usually die of natural causes.

In hockey the derrière is the one part of the body that may be used as a defensive weapon without violating the Geneva Convention. An army marches on its stomach, and a hockey team retreats on its bottom. Dorsal dexterity can take a player all the way to the Hockey Hall of Fame, where posterity will gaze upon his asset cast in bronze.

Does the front of the body have no purpose in hockey? Indeed it does. It is the front of the uniform that bears the club insignia. This identification is vital in that it reduces the chance of a player's being flattened by a teammate. Regardless of how brilliant a back end he has, every player should straighten up from time to time to identify himself for the benefit of both teams.

Stopping a breakaway

Fighting

Hitting sometimes leads to fighting, much as spring sometimes leads to summer.

Because hockey is a contact sport in which the contact can be of the same order as that of two freight trains approaching one another on the same track, a player may get the impression that he has been contacted too vigorously. The suspicion is often strengthened by his finding that he is having oral intercourse with an elbow not his own.

The frequent response to these intimations is to start a fight with the offending opponent by putting up the dukes. (Note: putting up a duke should not be confused with putting on a deke. You can put a deke on a goalie, but if you put a duke on a goalie his teammates will ensure that you wake up in post-op with even your hair in traction.)

Unlike other kinds of fighting—kung-fu, for example, or The Punic Wars—the hockey fight consists of throwing punches at the head. A player who throws a punch below the neck is considered to have struck a low blow since that is the location of the hockey player's main centres for shopping and entertainment. A player who punches an opponent in the stomach is unlikely to be invited into any future fights.

Because it is difficult to throw punches while on skates, the next phase of the fight is that of falling down. Here it is preferable to fall on top of your opponent rather than to have him fall on top of you, not only because a water mattress is a lot harder when it is frozen, but also because you have the temporary status of the missionary position that older spectators associate with manliness.

It is at this stage of the hockey fight that the linesmen intervene to prevent bad feeling. The linesmen, who are the two officials on the ice who are not the referee, have this additional responsibility of breaking up a fight as soon as it is evident that nobody is going to be seriously hurt. At a signal audible only to linesmen and dogs, each linesman grabs a combatant in a bunny hug, taking care not to seem to enjoy it too much. At this point in the fight, the player with the longer arms has a slight advantage as he can throw a punch that clears the ears of both linesmen and lands on the ear of the opponent whose arms are being held to prevent injury to himself. The player with very short arms, on the other hand (or indeed both hands), is destined to spend most of his hockey-fight career hitting linesmen on the back of the head and breaking his knuckles.

To help the short-armed player, every professional team has at least one player who acts as "policeman" (on a female team, "policewoman"). This player has arms so long that his knuckles brush his knees when he walks. Although the team policeman is not allowed to blow a whistle or shoot tear gas, he does carry the only riot stick in the world that comes up to the chin—several times, if necessary.

When he sees one of the smaller, more valuable members of the team getting into a fight, the policeman's job is to barge into the opponent and inform him that he has joined the meeting because he has a proxy vote on the relocation of his nose. His timing must be exquisite, however, because if he rushes to the rescue after the fight has started he becomes the "third man in" and may be given a game misconduct. It is better, therefore, to err on the side of arriving too soon, and a good team policeman will ignore the puck in order to concentrate on hostile vibrations—the trading of dirty looks between players who "have got something going"—so that he may get an early start at proving that an ounce of prevention is worth a pound in the ear.

Despite the policeman and the linesmen, a fight sometimes gets out of hand and results in "clearing the benches," when all the players grab a partner and reproduce a Roman orgy scene without the grapes. The fight then enters its final phase entitled "Remove Your Sweaters and See Who Has the Nicest Suspenders." This usually proves beyond doubt who is the better man.

Passing the Puck

Next to hitting and fighting, being able to pass the puck is useful. The less the player has the puck, the fewer times he gets hit and punched out. This does not mean that he should pass the puck to anybody who asks politely. The puck is passed to a teammate, whenever possible, while he is moving in the general direction of enemy lines. To avoid putting the other player off-side, the pass must be made with great precision, using the stick or the foot, but not the hand or any other appendage, however versatile.

The two basic passes in hockey are *passing in*, when the player centres the puck from the wing, and *passing out*, when the player loses all interest in the game.

Also crucial is the defenceman's ability to pass quickly to a forward and provide what is known as a *breakaway*. The term may cause some confusion among players who associate a breakaway with a type of gown worn by exotic dancers, especially when they hear a sportscaster say that a player has "undressed the defenceman." Hockey is not this kind of encounter group, however, and the person who engages in the sport hoping to see something he won't see in ping-pong is simply wasting everyone's time.

In hockey a breakaway is accomplished by a pass that enables the attacker to get behind the opposing defenceman, leaving nothing between the attacker and the goalie. (Note: occasionally there *is* something between the attacker and the goalie, if they have been room-mates as juniors, but the relationship should not affect the play.)

Passing to the player most advanced down ice is called "headmanning the puck" and is considered more effective than refusing to pass the puck to anyone or "hogging the puck." The reason: the player who is skating out of his own end has the better chance of putting the puck into a goal other than his own. Some players have trouble understanding the complexity of this pass. Perhaps because of some fundamental weakness in their sense of direction, instead of headmanning the puck they skate with it in tight circles, hoping that someone will take it away from them before they get dizzy and fall down. Or they may attempt a *drop pass*. This is a particularly helpful type of pass because it can be used by a player who accidentally leaves the puck behind him to make it look as though he intended it to be picked up by a following teammate. (See Chapter 5, "theatre arts.")

To be wholly convincing, however, a player should not attempt the drop pass unless he has good reason to believe that he is being followed by someone sympathetic to his mission. Unusually good peripheral vision is required for a player to see who is directly behind him. This is why passing is improved when players learn to "call for the puck."

How do you call for the puck? "Here, puck! Here, puck! That's a good boy, pucky...." No. Natural, but not clear. The player calling for the puck should be able to address the puck carrier by name. This brings us to a critical factor in passing the puck: knowing the names of the other players on the team. To know one's own name is an excellent beginning. But hockey is a game that tests endurance of mind as well as body. Because the action is so fast, it is simply not practical for the player to refer to the official program when he wants to know the name of the player from whom he wishes to call the puck. Indeed, the best professional players invent nicknames—names like "Flakey," "Shakey," or "Snakey"—as a kind of code.

They do *not* yell "Hey, you with the skin problem."

Besides knowing each other's names, a winning team often has what is called "a good holler guy." A good holler guy compensates for a lack of other skills by having a talented mouth. By helping to support the team morale he may even be voted Most Valuable Lip.

The aptitude for being a good holler guy is probably something a player is born with. ("Slap me again, Doc.") Hollering is best practiced at home and better still, if one is available, in a barn where the player can build up confidence in his utterance, avoid premature ejaculation, and learn to motivate the cows vocally before testing his holler on a human being.

A breakaway

Shooting

Ability to shout should be backed by ability to shoot. The player who depends on the opposition to knock the puck into its own net is leaning too hard on Lady Luck. Sooner or later he finds himself being handed the puck in front of an empty net. If he misses the net by several feet or "fans" on his shot (*cloutus interruptus*) he raises the suspicion that he is impotent.

Hockey players sometimes have numerous children in order to compensate for weakness in scoring elsewhere. The wife of a non-rushing defenceman may be pregnant much of the time unless he can be persuaded to take extra shooting practice. While no shame is attached to this deviate behaviour, the beginning player should consider that he does not gain financially from his prowess in activating the red light of the labour room. On the contrary, the price of kids' skates being what it is, he will be much better off concentrating on what it takes to penetrate the net.

Good shooting, then, occurs when energy is transferred from the stick to the puck in such a way that the puck is propelled into the goal, either directly or as a result of caroming off any object except the Queen Mother. Unless the player wishes to go to a great deal of trouble to dig a tunnel under the ice to the opposing goal, shooting the puck into it is the most reliable way of having it found there.

The shot may be the (a) wrist shot (b) slap shot or (c) buck shot (illegal).

First, the wrist shot. The player with a good wrist shot is esteemed because he has learned to use a part of his arm other than the elbow. (The junior player can locate his wrist by holding his hand in front of his face and following the thumb back to the place where his Mom took his Dad's pulse, after she told him how much the bill was for the partial denture.)

The beauty of the wrist shot lies in its quickness. Having quick wrists helps to make up for slowness in other parts of the body, such as the brain. Unlike the sport in which the climax is facilitated by foreplay (golf), hockey does not allow the player enough time to take several practice swings, unless he wants to become part of the fairway.

The slap shot

The object in hockey is to consummate the act as quickly as possible. This what makes hockey the uniquely Canadian game it used to be.

The most popular shot in hockey is *the slap shot*—the idiot brother of the rubber bullet. In the slap shot accuracy is not as important as the brute force behind the puck which attains speeds of up to two hundred kilometres an hour and qualifies as NATO's only ground-to-air missile with no sense of direction at all.

The wrist shot

Because it requires a rather long backswing, the slap shot is fired from well outside any populated area. The "point" (that desolate region near the blue line) is a favourite site for launching the slap shot. If the puck is rolling on edge when the slap shot is applied, it may take an erratic flight that could hasten the goalie's appointment with a psychiatrist.

To heighten further the element of suspense for the goalkeeper, the player may delay his slap shot till some of his teammates have created a crowd scene in front of the goal, whereupon the slap shot becomes a *screen shot*. The screen shot is often described by the sportscaster as "going through a maze of players." This gives the play a bit of Old-World charm. The picture of Puck, the unpredictable, tripping gaily through the maze, plucking an ear here, an eyebrow there, recalls a midsummer nightmare.

Regardless of the fickle course of a shot, a player never scores accidentally. He scores on *a deflection*. The seasoned hockey player is always ready to take credit for the deflection. He does not show surprise, have a fit of the giggles, or otherwise indicate that there was anything unexpected about the shot that bounced off his chin. (Note: a *deflection* should not be confused with a *defection*, which is what Canadian hockey coaches hope that Russian and Czech hockey players will attempt while visiting Canada.)

5/TACTICS (THE 32 POSITIONS)

Backchecking

eing able to hit, fight, pass, shoot, and blow bubble gum are the basic skills of hockey. But to win, a team must combine these skills with techniques of playmaking that at one time were considered to be unnatural. Today these are seen to be part of the joy of hockey.

The Power Play

A good coach knows that his team has a better chance of scoring when his team has more men on the ice. For example, if he has six men playing against five, or better yet against four, he has what is known professionally as "the advantage." His team may be scored against while it has the advantage—a "short-handed goal"—but this is the exception to the rule that it is desirable to outnumber the opposition.

When the team has a numerical advantage, it employs a special system called "the power play." The power play is like a gang rape except that there are only two minutes in which to overcome resistance. (Five minutes, on special occasions.) On the power play the attacking players pass the puck around between them until the defenders become moody about never having it and make a mistake.

The attackers then work the puck into "the slot."

The slot is the most sensitive area in an opponent's end. The beginning player is often unable to find the slot and is too shy to ask where it is. Actually, the slot is the frontal approach to the goal. The experienced hockey player may not be able to describe its exact location, but he always knows when he is in it.

On the power play he may succeed where others have failed because he is working under less crowded conditions. However, he should be properly grateful for the opportunity, particularly if he picks up the puck on the rebound, when it is susceptible. The player risks getting the reputation of collecting "garbage" goals, and nobody wants to be known as a garbageman in hockey, if for no other reason than that it puts extra strain on his deodorant.

Killing the Penalty

When the referee gives the wrong team the advantage of the power play, a player may be called upon to help "kill the penalty." In Canada, killing the penalty is one kind of execution that does not require approval by the federal cabinet.

Penalty killing is such a specialized skill that some players are used only when their side is short-handed. The coach can build up the confidence of such a player by letting him believe that it is normal to have only four teammates with him on the ice. Disillusionment comes soon enough in life. Once a player realizes that he is playing for two, he may develop a split personality, want two numbers, order double portions in restaurants, and otherwise add to the club's overhead.

The penalty killer must excel in "checking"—which is like hitting but without the falling down—and "ragging the puck." What is ragging the puck? Ragging the puck is skating in circles at mid-ice, not doing anything with the puck and not letting anyone else do anything with it. The purpose of this manoeuver is to kill time. When this is well done, the crowd applauds wildly, proving that Canadians would sooner watch time being wasted than have no leisure activity at all.

The really deft penalty killer may even "steal the puck." This does not mean that he puts the puck into his pocket while the referee isn't looking. (The only times the player is allowed to pocket a puck are (a) when he wants a souvenir of his one-hundredth, two-hundredth, three-hundredth, etc., career goal (b) when he is too cheap to buy his kid a Christmas present.)

By stealing the puck the penalty killer may score a short-handed goal, which is roughly equivalent to the defeat of the Spanish Armada. Even if he does not score a short-handed goal, the accomplished penalty killer can provoke an opponent into a desperation move that can be embellished into an off-setting penalty. This brings us to the cultural influence of hockey as one of—

The Theatre Arts

Not only the penalty killer but all the players on the team, including the goalkeeper, must be proficient actors. "All the world's a stage," said the father of modern comedy (Eddie Shack). Nowhere is the artistic side of hockey more developed than in Canada, though Russian hockey players are almost as sublime, with their great tradition of Boom-Boom Chekhov, Go-Go Gogol, and the Bolshoi Ice Follies.

Le Pas de Dive

Every hockey player should be able to perform the dive, no matter how much water is on the ice. The virtuoso can turn a clumsy trip over an opponent's stick into a deliberate act of treachery by the foe by pitching to the prone position like the fatally fouled Hamlet. ("Now cracks a noble heart.")

Of course the dive is lost as a thing of beauty unless the referee sees it. Beauty does not exist in hockey unless it is observed by an official. For this reason, the player taking the dive should utter a cry of some kind—"Curse thee, varlet"— or should display the following—

Creative Bleeding

For most journeymen hockey players the effective way to portray the victim of unprovoked brutality is to bleed. A good bleeder is indeed a pearl. The two-minute penalty for slashing or elbowing is raised automatically to five minutes if the player whose face has been in the neighbourhood of the assault shows that blood has been drawn. If the game is being televised, the player should bleed on camera. (He can tell by the red light on the camera which one is transmitting the picture.) The referee will not hesi-

tate to assess the major penalty when a bleeding player is rapidly creating a gory puddle on the ice that will have to be scraped up by the linesmen, delaying the game and marring the TV commercial for Heinz ketchup.

Should the bleeding be scripted, as in professional wrestling? This question is often asked by players who would prefer their broken jaw wired shut for Lent rather than during Christmas. Regrettably, the answer is negative. What crowds—and particularly American crowds—find refreshing about hockey violence is that it is improvisational theatre, a change from the well-made play crafted by such dramaturges as Strangler Lewis and Haystack McGoon.

The gladiatorial contest loses something of its impact when one of the brawlers misses his cue and his fellow combatant must fill in with the equivalent of a soft-shoe dance. Formal theatre is found in—

The Masque and the Renaissance

The best of costume drama in hockey is that performed by the goalkeeper: the masque. As in a Greek tragedy, the goalie's masque allows him to express great agony after stopping a shot and when his team needs a breather. The masque is allegorical, depicting the wounding of Good by Evil, followed by a miraculous recovery when the goalie sees the back-up goalie coming off the bench.

The netminder's costume has a rich potential for holding up play at critical junctures. Braces, straps, buttons, pads—any of these may create an equipment problem requiring the goalie to skate to the bench very slowly (holding his pants up) to receive attention. Although referees have been less appreciative of the goalie's sartorial crises in recent years, no official will wave play on if all the goalie's gear self-destructs and leaves him standing in his thermal underwear, or worse.

Foldout deke

Deking

When we hear that a hockey player has "undressed" a
defenceman, the word is usually used in a figurative
sense. It describes a movement by the puck carrier that
fools the defending player so completely that he wishes
he had moved to Tonga. This is called "putting a move
on" the defender and can lead to a goal if the player can
do it without shortening one leg in the process. Various
parts of the body may be used to put the move on an opponent: the hip fake, the shoulder fake, the head fake,
and the teeth fake (the denture flies out of the mouth in a
misleading direction, preferably with a mocking grin).

When the move is put on the goalkeeper it is called a
"deke," after Donald Deke, who was better known as a
realtor.

The Penalty Shot

A player has a golden opportunity to deke the goalie when the referee awards him a penalty shot, though this does not happen often enough to replace "the bread-and-butter play" (bread-and-butter sticks to the stick better than the puck).

The penalty shot is awarded when the player attacking is "in the clear" in the opposing end and is hauled down from behind by a defender using a lasso or other questionable means. The player on the penalty shot has an uninhibited chance to put the puck past the goalie, and his solo rush is one of the most exciting plays in hockey, providing he remembers to pick up the puck. Surprisingly, often the goalie foils the attempt, fending off the best deke the attacker can put on him, and this is one of the leading causes of thumb-sucking among players.

Goalkeeping

Goalkeepers have different styles, which is okay as long as the goalie doesn't show up for practice in high-heeled skates. Two distinguishable styles are those of the "stand-up" goalie and the "floppy" goalie. The beginning goalie tends to flop a great deal as he is under the impression that his players will have a better average if he spends a lot of time on his knees.

Coaches encourage the floppy goalie to become a stand-up goalie because if the defencemen see their goalie lying on the ice a lot they want to lie down too, either by throwing themselves in front of a shot or simply curling up with a good book. By remaining upright on his skates the goalkeeper not only provides a good example to his teammates but also retains his mobility in case he wishes to skate behind his net to attack the goal judge.

In his intimate relationship with the ice, the goalie establishes his superiority by abusing it at the start of each period, lacerating it with his skates, and glaring it into submission. The only instance of sado-masochism in hockey, the goalie's affair with his crease should not deter the ordinary, clean-living Canadian lad from considering this position in order to know the ecstasy of the game. Better to have played hockey and roughed up the ice than never to have loved at all.

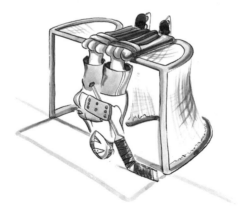

6/SHOULD YOU TAKE MONEY FOR IT?

lthough European philosophers have argued for centuries about the purpose of life, in Canada this is well established. For any God-fearing young Canadian the ultimate reward is to be chosen for the NHL All-Star Game. If he later goes to Heaven, that is so much gravy. The main thing is to avoid the fate of the damned—being sent down to Tulsa, or Rochester, or other of the nether regions (the Hockey Styx).

The promising player must decide, therefore, whether he wants to play hockey just for fun, as an amateur receiving no remuneration, or if he wants his parents ever to speak to him again.

Junior Hockey

How old should a child be before he starts playing hockey? While some coaches like to begin working with the player during the pre-natal period—mostly a matter of urging the foetus to thump its mother in the corners—it is probably more practical to wait for the post-partem slap shot, when the bouncing baby boy can be trapped on the rebound and handed a stick.

Will a boy grow up bowlegged if put on skates before he has learned to walk? Possibly, but bowlegs can be corrected easily by having the child sleep with his legs in a stove pipe. In any event, being bowlegged is not altogether a bad thing in a game where the player spends a good deal of his time bracketing the blue line.

In the matter of early environment there is no question that the junior hockey player raised on a prairie farm has a distinct edge. Thanks to the outhouse, he learns to move very fast on ice before he acquires skates. Owning the indomitable legs of a Gordie Howe is simply not compatible with indoor plumbing. Today, even the rural home is so fully equipped with modern conveniences that a youngster's stamina is lost to the septic tank. If it is true, as some critics say, that the world's fastest game is slowing down, it may be the result of young North Americans being deprived of the opportunity to run five miles to school every day. The urban parent who is ambitious for his child as a future hockey star will therefore enroll him in a school outside city limits and persuade him that the school bus is an instrument of the Devil.

Before he runs to school every day, the junior will have spent an hour or so in practice at the ice rink. Because of the heavy demand for ice time, this practice is usually scheduled for five or six A.M. This is why it is easy to recognize the parent of the junior hockey player: he has blue circles under his eyes and it is a big night when he stays up late enough to watch the seven o'clock news.

Should a child be made to go to his hockey practice if

he doesn't want to? Parents are often distressed by this crisis in the family, which can take the form of the child's using his hockey kitbag to pack his things and run away from home. A father may become even more upset when his son tells him that he would sooner practice the violin because the hours are better.

Parents, however, should try not to use force in getting the child out to hockey practice. For one thing, it may disturb sleeping neighbours if the lad's screams are heard as he is being frog-marched to the car in the pre-dawn darkness.

Instead, try the positive approach, convincing the youngster that—

(a) the pre-dawn darkness is the shank of the morning—nothing of any consequence happens after sunrise.

(b) should the little chap fall asleep over his French homework, Daddy will do it for him and if necessary take Miss Latulippe out to lunch.

(c) yes, it is too bad that he will miss his grannie's funeral, but the old lady showed bad timing by dying during the playoffs.

(d) no, Timothy's mother was wrong when she told him that there are other things in life besides hockey. What she was probably thinking of was things like eating, sleeping, and going to the bathroom, but this is how women look at life.

(e) there is nothing nutritionally wrong with eating

three breakfasts. Too much oatmeal never hurt anybody, regardless of what the doctor said about his lumpy complexion.

(f) if God had intended the junior hockey player to play other games besides hockey He would not have created the hockey coach.

The parent's relationship with his son's coach is the most delicate of all human intercourse. It is rich in ambivalence. That is, the parent must admire a man who serves his community by giving so many hours to acting as mentor to a group of youngsters who otherwise might be out on the street enjoying themselves. On the other hand, he has to wonder about a guy who chooses to spend much of his time with young boys. His immense gratitude to the coach is haunted by stories he has heard about scoutmasters who awarded merit badges for an activity not envisaged by Lord Baden-Powell.

The only way for the parent to escape this quandary is to become a coach himself, and even then he may wonder. The hockey peewee who is coached by his own father also faces special problems, but he must try hard to understand that his father finds it easier to be suspected of nepotism than pederasty. Also, the peewee can tell his teammates that the coach is not his real father but just someone his mother lives with till the Memorial Cup.

Whether or not he is related to him, the young player should find a coach who is a low-key person and who can keep a tight control on his reaction to his team's performance during the game, unless the team loses, in which case he shoots himself. This spares the parents a messy job.

Much has been said and written about parents and coaches using the youngster as an extension of their own egos, resulting in the child being put under so much adult pressure that if his team loses he bursts into tears. Let us examine this criticism clinically. Is it, after all, altogether unhealthy for a child to have a good cry? We live in an era of liberation in which women urge men to allow the emotions access to the floodgates of the lachrymal glands. If the father is weeping after the hockey game, and the coach is weeping, what is more natural than the youngster's joining in and sobbing his little heart out?

This does not mean that there may not be a period during which the junior leaguer can play hockey as a mere pastime—till he is, say, four. To prolong childish pleasures beyond this age is to run the risk of making a permanent fetish of one of the most repugnant perversions in hockey:

A Good Loser

We have put the phrase in Olde English type in keeping with the tradition of losing gracefully, which was something taught in British private schools to boys of the upper class who could afford to smile at losing a game since their fathers owned most of India.

It was part of their noblesse oblige, a French expression meaning "We have let you score more goals than we did, but your mother wears army boots."

Certainly, however, there is no place for a good loser in Canadian hockey. If the teams shake hands after the game it is, as every good coach knows, because it is the last chance to break an opponent's thumb. Almost as pernicious as a good loser is:

A Poor Winner

Some misguided individuals believe that the members of the winning team—especially if the score was lopsided—should not crow over their crushed rivals by sticking their tongues out at them, distributing crying towels, or otherwise "rubbing it in." Nonsense! Inhibiting the natural instinct to gloat may be harmful to a hockey player's personal development and also may encourage zits.

Instead, the player should make the most of his moment as a poor winner by expressing himself in a victory dance after scoring a goal. The choreography is built around the basic ballet movement of raising the arms and hockey stick high into the air. The next compulsory figure is for the goal scorer to skate up to the teammate who passed him the puck and embrace him whereupon both players skate to the teammate responsible for the other assist and leap into his arms. Whether the goal scorer kisses his teammates depends to some extent on his finding the fine line between being merely demonstrative and changing the game to restricted adult entertainment.

Since the feminist movement has made men more insecure about their physical contact with females, there has been an increase in the attention that male athletes pay to one another during the heat of the game. Bottom-patting, waist-hugging, and hair-ruffling are rife and usually evolve into one or two incidents of players rolling around in a large, passionate mass that the officials are reluctant to try to separate.

A safe rule for this kind of fray: if you wouldn't do it in a steam bath, don't do it on the ice.

Rather than allowing his scoring a goal to arouse him to intimate relations with his linemates, the player should practice a brief, solo dance of triumph that is exhibitionistic without being explicitly sexy. Quick little steps, a leg kick, a pirouette—any of these may be used, as long as they do not expand into a free-skating routine better left to Toller Cranston.

However a winning score is celebrated, the main point to remember is that concern for the defeated players' sensibilities is morbid and will deprive them of the chance to develop character in adversity. The NHL rule book makes it clear that any conduct is permissible toward a fallen foe with the exception of carrying off his women as slaves.

Some mention should be made here of one of hockey's more hazardous women: *the hockey mother.* The mother who is a single parent, or who is married to someone who makes her feel like a single parent, sometimes takes excessive interest in the career of the young hockey player in the family, in much the same way that the sow grizzly takes an interest in anyone that comes between her and her cub when the cub is not getting enough ice time.

The best thing to do if you are a young player with a hockey mother is to have a sister. The mother can get even more protective toward a daughter who is a figure skater than toward a son who is a hockey player, since she can't make short, frilly skirts to set off her son's drilling himself into the ice.

Having a sister, however, usually requires the co-operation of the boy's father, if he can be found. If the father cannot be found, or is too far into tennis, the player's coach should be prepared to make a few sacrifices for the good of the team.

Professional Hockey

While he is still a junior, the player may be approached by scouts of professional teams seeking out toddlers interested in making a career of the game. In fact, of the middle-aged men in long overcoats seen hanging around the kindergarten annex, only a small percentage are sexual molesters. The rest are pro hockey scouts.

The professional leagues have been faulted for recruiting hockey players too young to understand that signing an NHL contract is not really a substitute for learning bladder control. The critics accuse the big leagues of bribing beardless youths into a life of enforced labour and of being the only white slavers whose camel route passes through Flin Flon, Manitoba.

Others blame the pros for the too-much-too-soon syndrome—the disastrous effects of the sudden change from an allowance of two dollars and fifty cents a week to a hundred and fifty thousand dollar yearly income, plus the gift of a new automobile and bonus money if he remembers to wash behind his ears. With sudden wealth lavished upon him, the lad is tempted to squander it on expensive luxuries: race horses, fancy women, a small farm in Ontario.

It is important to help the young person to keep both feet on the ground. On the other hand, too much ballast may prevent him from getting off the ground at all. Most parents of the young, talented hockey player, therefore, prefer to look upon his sudden commercial success as an act of God: if they trespass against it, theirs will be the only house in the block afflicted by a plague of locusts.

The Draft

Although the degree of violence is not dissimilar, to be drafted for World War III is less satisfying than to be drafted by the NHL. The annual ceremony of the draft is, in fact, a major spring harvest in Canada, second in value only to the rape crop. One day, the rustic rite may well rival the ancient European festival of the Corn-maiden and include the symbolic slaughter of an NHL general manager to propitiate the crop of rookies.

Since the juniors are chosen in order of desirability, it is better for the player to be a first-round draft choice than, say, a thirty-second-round draft choice. The thirty-second-round draft choice should definitely review his plans for having his closet enlarged to hold a dozen two-hundred-dollar suits.

The junior who is not drafted at all is known as a "free agent." Some parents have great difficulty accepting that they have a son who is a known free agent, especially if they have a daughter who is a known hooker. It can be the final blow. To comfort them, and himself, the free agent should think of himself as among the late bloomers—those hockey players who may be thirty years old before they become the sensation of training camp. If he has failed to bloom by the time he is fifty, however, it may be sensible to tell his parents that they should unpack their bags as their trip to Tahiti is in doubt.

Because the pro team at the bottom of the league

gets first-draft choice (unless it has given it away to another team), the best young players go to the worst teams. The worst teams are usually those which are in financial difficulty as a result of drawing crowds so small that the usherettes draw isolation pay. For this reason, the junior should show his delight at being drafted by a loser by swallowing his tongue. He is then unable to speak except through—

The Agent

Some sociologists believe that it is deleterious for the young hockey player to go straight from his mother's arms to his agent's tentacles without first spending a year or two supported by nothing but his jockstrap. The suggestion is not realistic. The drafted player who lets his mother do the negotiating for his contract may save some money in agent's fees, but often he is stuck with an agreement that places undue emphasis on the responsibility of the coach to make sure that he wears mittens on the road and to tuck him in at bedtime.

A professional agent is preferable, therefore, regardless of whether he makes good peanut-butter cookies. The player cannot have everything, and his relationship with his agent is vital to his success in pro hockey. The player may also take a wife, but, when he speaks of the person he would trust in a hotel room with the team's manager, he means his agent.

How does a player choose a good agent? First, a good agent is likely to be more expensive than the agent who shares his phone with a car wash. When the player reads the fine print on his contract, he may discover too late, if his agent is unreliable, that he has signed away his right to eat anything but Sugar Smacks, the Breakfast of Chumps.

Product endorsements provide additional revenue that can exceed what the pro hockey player earns playing hockey. Therefore, it is important for him to have an agent who knows how much the traffic will bear in pantyhose, power tools, and other products for home and industry. Millions of youngsters look up to the pro hockey player as a kind of demigod, and this makes it imperative that the player have an agent who will guide him away from certain types of product identification such as a TV commercial for soap. Even such apparently innocuous endorsements as shaking hands with a used-car dealer may hurt the player's image, unless the used-car dealer is under treatment for leprosy.

Besides counselling the player on the sale of T-shirts and foot fungicides, the good agent often serves as an investment advisor, persuading the young pro that the signing bonus of one hundred thousand dollars makes for too lumpy a mattress. Some players have had this trust abused by an agent who took their hard-earned cash—including that for posing in all-wool cardigans that are right for today's man of action—and, instead of investing the money wisely, moved it into his Swiss bank account under the cover of being an exporter of powdered yodel. In spite of such occasional irregularity, the pro hockey player is better off with an agent than trying to handle his money matters himself. When he jumps over the boards on a line change, the player does not want to have his mind occupied with whether a five-year term deposit at 9.5 per cent has a yield after taxes superior to that of a 5 per cent discount bond selling at eighty-three dollars. With his mind so occupied, the player may not only put himself off-side but also may forget to put on his pants.

The Players' Association

In addition to placing himself in the hands of an agent, the hockey pro will want to join the players' association—the only labour union in the world whose brothers club one another in the name of solidarity.

It is sometimes asked how it is possible for a hockey player to be a loyal member of the association and at the same time throw a bodycheck that could put a fellow member into the orthopedic ward. The answer to this is that in hockey the brotherhood of the working class is very strong except during the Stanley Cup playoffs, when it becomes back-up to the law of the jungle.

7/THE MYSTIQUE OF HOCKEY

n Canada the Holy Grail of sport is the Stanley Cup. The Grey Cup may have superior powers with respect to the amount of damage done to hotel rooms in its name, but the Stanley Cup is at the centre of a major spring festival that has replaced Easter as the time when people toss eggs onto the ice. This is also the longest festival, as the Cup runneth over from April into May.

As we all know, the Stanley Cup is very old, having been donated by a British governor general (Lord Stanley of Stanley Park) as a symbol of his gratitude for being allowed to leave Canada without having his baggage inspected. The addition of names of winning teams has built up the trophy till it is now as tall as some of the players that tote it in triumph around the arena. Soon the Stanley Cup will have to be put on wheels, despite the risk that hockey fanatics may hurl themselves to death under the juggernaut.

The purpose of the Stanley Cup playoffs is to find out which team is the best. Of course the point standings at the end of the regular season already have shown which team is the best, but these don't count. In the sacred rites of the NHL, confirmation is most beloved by Providence.

During the Stanley Cup playoffs the player has extraordinary demands put on his finesse in—

Meeting the Media

In their desperate hunt for copy, sportscasters and press reporters seek out players before games, after games, and between periods; till he lifts the lid the player cannot be sure that he is alone in the bathroom.

The pro must be prepared, therefore, to sit down at any moment, perspiration dripping off his nose, and be interviewed about the reason why his team is behind ten to one. Following, in order of importance, are some helpful hints for players being interviewed:

Take a Towel

TV viewers are glad to see a player's face streaked with honest blood, sweat, and tears, but not if he wipes it on his sleeve. Mothers who are watching would see it as a bad example for the kids whose laundry they do. Carry a towel at all times, therefore, remembering that a white towel is more appropriate for formal occasions. Never be interviewed holding a towel stolen from a hotel room, unless your name happens to be Royal York.

Also, take care that in your personal appearances before the camera and at club banquets you wear a nice, conservative suit and necktie and have your hair shining

clean and styled to cover the place where your ear was. On no account should a hockey player do an interview without his teeth in. The viewing public cherishes the illusion that playing hockey is compatible with biting an apple. Gaping evidence to the contrary casts a pall over the TV interview or the luncheon address, and the player whose jaw has been wired shut should accept no public speaking engagements at all, unless he has very expressive eyes.

Praise the Opposition

Regardless of your private opinion that the team you are playing against is made up of players overdue to be picked up by the pound, be lavish in your praise of the opposition. The first commandment of the media is: Thou shalt not put down thine enemy with the jaw of a smart ass. The second commandment is: Thou shalt not take credit for your own success, but shall pay homage to thine teammates, even unto the stick boy.

A becoming modesty during interviews is essential to the hockey player, no matter how hard he has to work at it. Standing in front of the bathroom mirror and practicing the self-effacing grin is sometimes useful. No one expects the player to blush demurely when he is lauded on camera, but at the very least he should avoid nodding agreement or, worse, taking a bow. The following will serve as a model for the hockey interview:

INT: Bobby, you already have fifty goals this season. How do you account for this great start?

BOB: Well, Bill, uh, I feel that I've been very lucky.

INT: Lucky in what way, Bobby?

BOB: Well, uh, I've been lucky to be playing on a great line, with, uh, those two guys that are on the forward line with me. I've also been lucky that we got such great defencemen putting the puck on my stick and a couple of great goalkeepers.

INT: How do the goalkeepers help you score goals, Bobby?

BOB: Well, they're great holler guys, you know? They holler things like, uh, "Score another goal, Bobby!" and "God bless you, Bobby!"—things like that. When you're rushing up the ice, it's great to know that your goalie is behind you.

INT: A real boost.

BOB: I'm also lucky to have a great coach, who treats me like I was just a human being. And our general manager has a great organization, and the fans have been just great, in what to me is a really great town and a great country—the United States of Canada.

INT: America.

BOB: Wherever.

INT: And you hope to keep up the torrid pace in scoring goals?

BOB: Uh, I sure hope to keep up the torrid pace in scoring goals, Bill, so long as I have the good Lord out there with me laying on the body. . . .

In addition to rejecting the crown of glory, the hockey Caesar will familiarize himself with the jargon of the media, teaching himself to communicate in terms approved by the hot-stove league. As an exercise, he might choose the correct word or phrase to complete the following statements:

1. Our goalie is holding (a) a hot hand (b) a hot foot (c) a cold nose.

2. Our team has lost its last twelve games, but tonight when we play Toronto we hope to (a) turn over a new Leaf (b) turn invisible (c) turn it around.

3. When your team plays another team in the same division it is (a) a four-footer (b) a four-pointer (c) a form of incest.

4. You can tell a winning team by the way it keeps its (a) poise (b) old string (c) dental appointments.

5. A team will be heavily scored on if the defencemen have a habit of (a) gagging on their bubble gum (b) coughing up the puck (c) gargling their aftershave.

6. A puck shot directly at the net is (a) labelled (b) libelled (c) posted for next-day delivery.

7. The player whose last goal was in October 1974 is in (a) a filthy mood (b) a scoring slump (c) a city dump.

8. The player who bowls over everything in his path is said to have (a) come to play (b) come to in hospital (c) come to me, my melancholy baby.

9. It is the ambition of every netminder to have a sparkling (a) wine (b) gem in his navel (c) goals-against average.

10. The team that has qualified for the Stanley Cup playoffs is accorded (a) a standing ovation (b) a sitting ovation (c) a matched set of horseshoes.

The Organ

To comprehend the mystique of hockey we must consider for a moment the role of the organ. Some young players want to know about the organ but are afraid to ask. Playing with the organ, is, however, a vital part of the joy of hockey. Indeed, were it not for the stimulation of the organ, the degree of excitement experienced by the crowd would be much reduced, particularly in cities like Vancouver and Los Angeles where arousal is cooled by the Japanese Current.

Where is the organ situated? No hockey player should be ashamed to discuss this. Usually, the organ is concealed from public gaze because its function conforms to the Canadian ideal of creating a climax without attracting attention.

The organ also accompanies the soloist in singing the national anthem before the game. When they finish together, it is a rare moment of bliss—one to be respected by every young hockey player who aspires to organism.

Clean Living on the Road

Professional hockey players are obliged to spend days, sometimes weeks, on the road away from their mothers, wives, and sweethearts and exposed to Temptation. Very often the players stay at a hotel or, worse, a motel. For some Canadian boys this is their first experience of sleeping in a room where their Moms can't hear if the bed collapses. It is a severe test of character. The player sees the phone number for room service, and he may be seized by a strong impulse to have something sent up. It may only be a glass of water. But once a young man gets into the habit of having something sent up by room service, his mind becomes the Devil's playground.

Being in their sexual prime, hockey players can become aroused merely by the thought of an interlocking schedule. To counteract the immoral influence of road trips, the coach instructs his players in the following facts of life:

• The population of the city the team is visiting is 100 per cent male. Especially in Philadelphia. What appear to be women in the crowd are actually female impersonators.

• If the player on the road sees what he is convinced is a woman—a Bunny in a Playboy Club, for example—he must dismiss it as a mirage. These mirages are common in hot regions such as New York discos and California tennis courts and are caused by thermal radiation distorting the figure of what is, in fact, a truck driver.

• Another popular hallucination is that attractive young females called hockey "groupies" may manifest themselves outside the player's hotel room and offer him their combined amatory attention in exchange for an autographed puck. There is nothing sillier than the sight of a grown hockey player standing around expectantly in the hotel lobby, his pockets bulging with pucks on which he has laboriously printed his name. He should know that groupies are invariably women of low repute hired by the home team's management to keep the visiting player up past his bedtime and to add something to his milk and cookies that will cause him to play the next game entirely on his knees.

To be on the safe side, the pro hockey coach instills into his players the belief that any kind of sexual activity before a game impairs the player's performance on the ice. The same is true of sexual activity *after* a game. The only safe time is *during* the game. This is why the wife or girl-friend is encouraged to attend home games: she is available to blow her mate a kiss while his line is sitting on the bench and to dispel fantasies about how the referee would look in black net stockings.

The coach also impresses upon his players the teaching of St. Augustine that sex is not for recreation but for re-creation—of more hockey players. In this regard the Gordie Howe family is a glorious example of what God intended when He created the off-season.

The Hockey Hall of Fame

Canadians are not allowed to accept knighthoods or titles of nobility, but they can be elected to the Hockey Hall of Fame and use that as an excuse for wearing a wig.

Each year thousands of people pass through the

Hockey Hall of Fame not only because they revere the immortals of Canada's national game but because the queue is shorter than for Lenin's Tomb. Excavating the ruins of the Hockey Hall of Fame, archaeologists of the future will assume that Canadians buried their kings with their gold-plated hockey gear so that the soul of the departed sovereign could glide into the hereafter without having to rent skates.

This temple also serves as a shrine for one of the most treasured artifacts of professional hockey, namely:

Statistics

The main reason why every young player should try to obtain his high-school graduation is that he needs the math in order to grasp hockey statistics. Successfully memorizing the number on his sweater is not enough.

Although he is not as deeply into statistics as he would be if playing baseball or football—games which involve percentages that would give a Canadian player a nosebleed—hockey does place strong emphasis on the ability to add and subtract. The player may be known to his coach only as a plus or minus, depending on how many goals have been scored against the team while he was on the ice. Happiness is to be called a Plus Four. To be known as a Minus Six is a disgrace to the family and destructive of property values.

A quick line-change

Every professional club has its own statistician who uses computer technology to store the ever-growing mass of data that enables the coach to tell how well a player is doing without having to look at him. The coach bases his assessment on the simple formula of adding up the number of "hits" made by the player, subtracting his total penalty time, adding his career total of goals, subtracting his age, adding his pound weight (squared), subtracting his number of children (under six), and taking the total to the last place (the W.C.) to flush it down the tube so that the opposing coach will have to figure it out for himself.

Hockey has many other kinds of statistics besides the plus and minus. For example, the following:

(a) greatest number of goals scored in a single game

by a rookie with a red beard and a sister who entertains a lot

(b) the shortest interval between the two goals scored in a Stanley Cup playoff by a team short-handed by two players who both prefer their eggs sunny-side-up

(c) fewest number of penalties called in a game by a referee who has swallowed his whistle.

Without fascinating statistics such as these, the sportscaster would have nothing to talk about between periods and during dull, scrambly play, and he would develop deep emotional insecurity. Also, without statistics there would be no way of knowing when a player had established *a record*—the most exalted kind of statistic known to man.

The hockey record is enshrined in the Hockey Hall of Fame, where pilgrims may worship it till the record is broken, whereupon it is replaced by the new record while nobody is looking.

8/HOCKEY TOMORROW (OR TUESDAY AT THE LATEST)

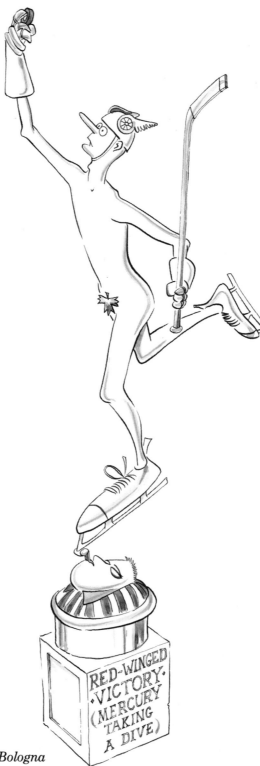

Apologies to Giovanni da Bologna

anadian hockey has been carried to all parts of the world, usually on a stretcher.

The game has been adopted with particular enthusiasm by communist countries such as the USSR, Czechoslovakia, and East Germany, as well as by the socialist countries of Scandinavia. As a result, hockey has been affected by state ownership of the puck and by the ideological belief that in the final stage of the game the referee will wither away.

European Hockey

European (or Un-Canadian) hockey is unfair because the players use tactics that make it much harder for a Canadian team to beat them, namely:

Foreign Skating

Europeans skate very fast so that when they play against Canadians they beat them to the puck. This is not very nice, considering how Canadian troops helped Europe during two world wars.

European hockey players not only show off by skating fast, they also don't get tired as quickly. The reason for this is that they practice on a larger ice surface (the Black Sea), with little or no regard for the fact that much of the Third World is desperately short of ice, to say nothing of mixer. European players also take drugs—aspirin, for example, when they have a headache. They spend an immoderate amount of time keeping in condition—time that Canadian players devote to a better-rounded program of walking to the bank and playing the stock market.

The Canadian player is superior at his own end of the awards dinner table. The Russian is adept with the puck but is weak at passing the sugar. He cannot give a funny dinner speech (in English); in fact he does not seem to say anything at all. His body has been developed at the expense of his vocal chords. Indeed, if we take the European hockey player off the ice he is really no match at all for the Canadian player.

Alien Puck Handling

European players are quick, accurate shooters and seriously reduce the element of luck that contributes so much to the pleasure of scoring a goal. The puck that goes straight from the stick into the net from a short distance is basically dull compared to the shot that takes a crazy bounce off the glass, hits the goalie on the back of the head, and drops behind him into the goal.

Fortunately, Swedish players brought into the NHL have shown a willingness to be retrained to take advantage of Divine Providence by firing the puck into a mass of players in front of the goal and praying for a miracle. Russian players, however, are hopeless. They have been indoctrinated to pass the puck around to one another, from each according to his abilities, to each according to his needs. They don't care how long this takes. In Russian hockey every rush is on The Five-Year Plan.

Deviate Penalties

European players take advantage of Canadian players in an international tournament by doing mean things for which Canadian hockey does not have penalties. Instead of normal relations such as charging, slashing, and cross-checking, the Europeans use biting, tickling, and kicking in the shin. Because these atrocities are not assessed as penalties, especially by European referees who have not learned the difference between a clean lobotomy and dirty hockey, Team Canada is provoked into acts of retaliation that result in losing players to the penalty box, in European press charges that Canadian hockey players are "hooligans," and in irreparable damage to Canada's reputation as a country blessed with natural immunity to civilization.

The question is, should Canadian players learn to

Pressure in the corners

turn the other cheek—never easy for young men with a good Christian upbringing—or should they adopt the sneaky tricks of the enemy and hope that these can be offset by giving regularly to the Salvation Army? The answer calls for some soul-searching. (The player should not attempt to search alone, but should consult a reliable gypsy or a church minister with a knowledge of spearing.)

Women's Hockey

Hockey is becoming more popular with women because it is one indoor game that they can play without being too worried about missing a period.

At this point in time (3:30 P.M.), the reaction of

most men to a mention of women's hockey is to snicker or to hide their true feelings by putting a shopping bag over their heads. This is a mistake. Any male who hoots at female hockey is apt to find that the wave of the future has caught him holding an anchor.

The reason for caution here is that more and more girls are taking up ice hockey, and they don't always wear their helmets to a party or a dance to warn a man in advance. Also it must be remembered that during certain vital years of adolescence—roughly from eleven to seventeen—girls today are bigger than boys. And have built-in padding. A boy who plays junior hockey would be wise, therefore, to stop laughing at female hockey players when he is ten and not start laughing again till he is twenty, or better yet eighty with a weakened desire to live.

Women's hockey can be as violent as men's except that the mayhem seems to be done in slow motion. Girls are exceptionally well endowed for face-scratching and hair-pulling, and in a fight the yanking of a sweater over a combatant's head could have such a dramatic effect on the crowd as to set men's hockey back about a hundred years.

If women players adapt their uniforms to a style borrowed from the costumes of ice chorines—tighter-fitting pants, a few ostrich feathers here and there—the competitive element of the game, already under attack by activists who stress participation over winning, will atrophy to the point where a team's most effective line will be the conga line.

What of mixed teams? Boys' teams have been ordered by the court to accept girls, to the satisfaction of parents who are relieved to have their daughter joining boys in an activity where she can only get knocked *down*.

When boys and girls are playing on the same hockey team, a girl is sometimes subject to anxious wondering—"If I make the first pass, will I lose his respect?" Her concern is not warranted. What the coach means when he tells his players to "get out there and grab two points" has nothing to do with the way a girl is built. A girl can hurt her team by refusing to go into the corners without a chaperone.

Fortunately, this old-fashioned type of girl is relatively rare in today's mixed hockey. A greater danger is posed by the opposite type: the girl who makes the team without going on the ice. The coach has a hint of such a female player when his boys show their best bursts of speed in sprinting for the showers.

The hockey club of mixed players faces the expense of providing separate locker-rooms, one for the girls, one for the boys, and one for the Don't Know. Most clubs cannot afford such duplicate facilities. Some have tried having one locker-room and turning out the light, but the mixed team that suits up in the dark runs special risks, not the least of which is having a lad skate onto the ice with a chin-strap by Wonder Bra.

Hockey in Space

Canada has been one of the pioneers in space hockey, having launched a man into orbit long before the Americans substituted the Saturn for Rocket Richard.

Canadian space scientists are ready, the moment a U.S. or Russian space lab becomes available, to test the effect of weightlessness on the slap shot. They see exciting possibilities in a puck deflecting into the goal off Mars.

Designs have been submitted already for the first "astronet." The astronet will be placed in stationary orbit above the Earth, with the astronetminder computerized to intercept the puck with a laser beam or his chin, whichever is closest.

Whether or not we shall be able to watch space hockey in our lifetimes, lovers of the game will be encouraged to know that the surface of planets like Saturn and Jupiter has been found to be mostly ice. The absence of life is no obstacle. If the NHL can expand to Cleveland, it can certainly support a franchise on Pluto.